Law of Attraction

Tested Secrets & Habits to Manifest Health, Happiness, Wealth & Unlimited Abundance in All Areas of Your Life

Law of Attraction Secrets Book 1

Copyright Maya Faro© 2016

All rights reserved. No part of this publication may be reproduced, stored in a retrieval system, or transmitted, in any form or by any means, electronic, mechanical, photocopying, recording or otherwise, without the prior written permission of the author and the publishers.

The scanning, uploading, and distribution of this book via the Internet or via any other means without the permission of the author is illegal and punishable by law. Please purchase only authorized electronic editions, and do not participate in or encourage electronic piracy of copyrighted materials.

Maya Faro © Copyright 2016 - All rights reserved.

Legal Notice:

This book is copyright protected. It for personal use only.

Table of Contents

Introduction 6

Chapter 1 11

Subconscious and Illusions of Reality 11

    Consciousness 12

    A World of Illusions 14

    Energy 16

    Thoughts 17

    Emotions 18

    The Power of Emotions to Attract 22

The Law of Attraction Mindset 26

Chapter 2 28

How to Remove Resistance 28

    Love and Appreciation 28

    Self-Love 29

    Values 30

    Whose Life Is It? 31

    Appreciation 34

    Meditation 36

    Emotional Diving 40

    Loving Yourself 42

    Journaling 43

    Visualizations 44

Affirmations 45

Chapter 3 46

Combining the Power of Emotion and Intention 46

    Intention 46

    Emotions 47

    How your Intentions affect Consciousness 48

Chapter 4 50

Putting the Pieces Together 50

Chapter 5 52

The Law of Attraction and Relationships 52

    Befriending your Unconscious Aspects 55

    Entering the Perspective of Another 57

Chapter 6 63

The Law of Attraction and Work 63

Chapter 7 71

The Law of Attraction and Money 71

    Chapter 8 80

    The Law of Attraction and Health 80

Chapter 9 87

Law of Attraction and Self-Improvement 87

    Chapter 10 90

    When the Law of Attraction Pulls the Rug From Under You 90

Chapter 11 95

Putting It All Together 95

    Exercise for Changing a Belief 97

    Create a Planner 100

Chapter 12 101

Sustaining the Effort 101

    Decision Making 102

    Support Group 103

Words of Encouragement 104

Introduction

Imagine a person who goes to a magical restaurant. This restaurant has no menu, and this person can order anything that they want to eat. All this person has to do is to imagine what they want to eat and the server will bring it to their table. Now imagine a different scenario. Another person goes to this same restaurant; however, this person is unsure of what they want to eat. Not only do they have trouble deciding on what they want to eat, but they also think of the foods that they do not want to eat. In this situation, the server brings every food that they thought of: The foods they like, the foods that they are unsure of, and the foods that gross them out.

The determining factors that caused these two scenarios to end so differently are focus and awareness. The first person focused on what they wanted, while the second person focused on whatever thought came to mind. Though not apparent in the scenarios, the level of awareness was another deciding factor, that is, the awareness of what was being focused on. The challenge that most of us face is that we are not aware of being aware. It is like the adage "The definition of insanity is doing the same thing over and over while expecting different results." Most of us have had experiences where we have mistaken our limited awareness for being the reality of the situation. An example of this limited awareness is when we try practicing a certain skill incorrectly. Imagine someone who is trying to learn to play tennis or golf without proper instruction. They continue to use incorrect form and get the same results. One day, they may come across someone who teaches them the correct form. Now, when they practice the proper form, they get new results and experience a greater awareness of how to play the game.

Awareness itself is unrestricted, unlimited, unchanging and constant. What does change is our ability to perceive the nature of our experience more clearly. Imagine if the sun and the moon were thinking beings. The moon may be thinking to itself "I am the one that creates the light that shines in the evening sky." The moon believes it is the one that generates light when it is the sun that is the source of light; the moon just reflects the light of the sun. We are not much different than the moon. The moon symbolizes our personal consciousness, while the sun represents our greater or universal consciousness. The sun's light is infinity greater than that which is being reflected by the moon. As long as we believe that we are just the "moon," we will have a limited view of reality. However, when we develop the knowing that we are the "sun," then we will come to know that our level of awareness is unlimited, as is our experience of reality.

Most of us believe that our minds are the source of awareness and that our experiences are objective reality. This belief is just as the moon believing it is the source of light. Awareness or consciousness is not created in the brain of each individual; rather, each one of us is like a cell phone tower that is picking up the signal of universal consciousness. Each person is creating their unique experience of reality that is based on the level of awareness that they are open to. What we are aware of is what we focus on, and what we focus on creates our reality. Contrary to what science exposes, reality is subjective rather than objective. There are an infinite number of realities, all of which are the expression of a single energy field that that contains infinite potential. It is this energy field that is the source of all existence, including consciousness. We expand our experience of reality when we develop greater awareness to the nature of consciousness. By understanding consciousness, we understand the Law of Attraction.

The Law of Attraction is an integral aspect of the universe; it is as natural as gravity. Everyone is utilizing the Law of Attraction to create their experience. The only difference between the two people who ate at the magical restaurant was that one of them understood how to utilize the Law while the other lacked awareness of it. In this book, we will explore the Law of Attraction, both in how it works as well as its application. Much of what will be discussed in this book goes against conventional knowledge and understanding. As mentioned earlier, there can be no experience without the awareness of it. Conventional knowledge and understanding, as well as unconventional knowledge and understanding, only exist because there is awareness of it. Rather than wondering what is true or untrue, reflect on how your life is unfolding. Are you getting everything that you ordered, or do you lack clarity as to what you are ordering? Either way, it will be brought to your table.

Free eBook + Newsletter

Before we jump into it, I would like to offer you a free complimentary book. I am a new author, and I am very grateful for you the reader. I would like to send you this short eBook as a token of appreciation. You will also get a chance to receive similar books (of my authorship as well as other authors') and new releases at massive discounts!

Sign up for free at:

www.YourWellnessBooks.com/affirmations

problems with your sign up?

Email: info@yourwellnessbooks.com

Chapter 1
Subconscious and Illusions of Reality

To effectively utilize the Law of Attraction, it is useful to have an understanding of consciousness, the mind, and how they both create our sense of experience. For most of us, we have a deep identification with our mind and body. How we experience ourselves and the world around us is informed by our thoughts, our five senses, and our physical body. If you are lying on a beach in Hawaii, you may have a thought: "This is so relaxing, the only thing I want to do is enjoy this great beach." Visually, you may be looking at the waves as they travel up the beach, the white sand, the people around you, and the blue sky above. You may be feeling the warmth of the sun and the softness of the sand, and you may be hearing the roar of the waves, the voices of other people, and the squawk of seabirds. You may smell the fresh and salty sea breeze or the smell of suntan lotion. If you are like most people, you will take these experiences as being real as they are happening to you.

We see experience happening to us because we see ourselves as being separate from the world around us. This sense of separation results in us basing our sense of identity on our experiences. If the experience of the world conforms to our expectations and desires, then we feel good about ourselves. If our experiences are not consistent with our expectations, we may become disappointed and experience self-doubt. Viewed from this perspective, our experience of life shapes our sense of identity. But what if this perspective is inaccurate? What if it is the other way around? Could it be that we create our experience?

Consciousness

The idea that we create our experience can be found in the many Eastern traditions, including Hinduism and Buddhism. A useful metaphor for the nature of consciousness is that of sleep. For most of us, what we experience in the waking state is taken to be real, while that which we experience in our dreams is considered unreal. In Hinduism and Buddhism, deep sleep is most real, while the waking state is the dream state.

To further understand this, let us first consider the state of deep sleep. The state of deep sleep is a state of pure consciousness as it is devoid of experience. While in deep sleep, we have no sense of our personal self, there are no thoughts, nor is there any sense of experience. When we are in deep sleep, everything that we know or experience vanishes. When we are in dream sleep, we experience ourselves as a character within the dream. Your character experiences the dream world in the same way as you experience yourself in waking life. In the dream, your character experiences itself as having thoughts, taking action, and experiencing feelings.

Further, your character sees itself as being separate from the other characters in the dream; your character sees "life" happening to it.

While the dream is occurring, your character's experience seems very real; however, it is just an illusion. Your dream character cannot think, take action, or have feelings. All of these qualities are just projections of your mind, the one who is having the dream. While dreaming, you create your experience, which is the dream, and you create yourself, the character in the dream. Why could not the same thing be occurring in our waking life? Could our waking life be just a dream as well? The truth of who we, at the most fundamental level, has an awareness of our mental functions, our bodily functions, and all of our experiences, including our dreams, and deep sleep. It is why many of the Eastern traditions believe that that deep sleep is our true state, while the dream and waking state are illusionary. The world of illusions is absent in deep sleep. Deep sleep is pure consciousness. The essential nature of who we are is not a physical body that has a mind. Our essential nature is consciousness, which expresses itself as a physical body and a mind.

Because our experience of ourselves is so closely associated with the mind and body, we have come to believe that we are the mind and body. This identification with the mind and body is so strong that our experience of the world, and ourselves, is filtered through them. Our sense of being a physical body creates the sense of separation between us and the rest of life. Our minds can only deal with information at a conceptual level, meaning that anything that is formless or metaphysical will not register. Because of this, all of our experience is perceived conceptually, meaning that we see it, touch it, hear it, or taste it. Anything that cannot be perceived conceptually is not recognized by the mind.

A World of Illusions

Quantum physics has demonstrated that the world of form and physicality is just an illusion, as is the atom. Newtonian physics taught us that all form is made of matter, that matter is the basic unit of life. Quantum physics has debunked that belief. Quantum physics has demonstrated matter is just a myth. The atom, which was once thought to be a solid mass, is now known to be void of any physical structure. The atom is just a fluctuation of energy. Our minds lead us to believe that we are separate entities unto ourselves that live in a world that is full of other physical beings and objects. The truth is that, at the quantum level, there is no form. Only at the level of the mind does a sense of separation and physicality exist. Any sense of form or physicality is a projection of our minds, just as we project ourselves into our dreams. At the quantum level, there is only energy and potentiality. At the quantum level, there is no difference between you, this book, and the furniture that you are sitting in. That which you desire to attract into your life exist there already; it is impossible for you to be separate from that which you desire.

Everything in the world that you experience as having form arises from that which is non-form, just as your dream character and its dream experience arise from your consciousness as you are sleeping. For the purpose of this book, we will refer to this non-form as consciousness. We hear terms such as consciousness, the sub-consciousness, the higher-self, and universal consciousness; however, they are all the same thing, just branded differently by our conceptual minds. The relationship between the different levels of consciousness can be illustrated by using the ocean as an example. Sunlight reaches only a certain depth in the ocean, after which the ocean world exists in perpetual darkness. The upper part of the ocean is illuminated while the lower level resides in darkness; however, there is only one ocean. Similarly, there are levels of consciousness that are filled with the light of our awareness, while the remaining levels are unknown to us. The conscious mind is the level that is illuminated by our awareness. The subconscious is the level of consciousness that the light of our awareness has yet to reach.

Every experience we have ever had in this lifetime, or past lifetimes, is maintained in the subconscious, including those memories that we are unable or unwilling to experience. These experiences were pushed from our conscious mind to our subconscious mind. When we have a belief or feeling that threatens our sense of self, we suppress it in our subconscious. In this way, the subconscious is acting as a guard to keep the conscious mind safe. Because of its unlimited capacity to retain experiences, the subconscious is the driving force for everything we do.

Energy

It was stated earlier that it is impossible for you to be separate from that which you desire. We will now discuss this in more detail. Since everything that exists is just energy, there is no such thing as separation. Everything that you have ever desired, or will desire, already exists within your life at this moment. At the level of normal human awareness, we see that which we desire as being separate from us. Because we feel that we need to obtain that which we desire to feel complete, our life's energy drops to a lower frequency, preventing that which we desire from entering our life. We only attract that which is of like energy.

Energies of same frequency attract each other, while energies of different frequencies repel each other. To understand the Law of Attraction, we need to understand the quality of the energy that we are giving off and how to change its frequency. The Law of Attraction is about frequency management. To understand frequency management, we first need to understand the nature of thoughts and emotions.

Thoughts

Everything exists as energy, and that energy expresses itself as physical phenomena. The physical phenomena that most influence our lives are our thoughts and emotions. Our thoughts create our experiences of reality. The meaning of any experience that you will ever have is the product of thought. Your thoughts determine what you place your focus on, how you evaluate things, the decisions that you make, and the action you take. Our thoughts also create our experience of reality at even deeper levels. We can illustrate this using a rose. When you look at a rose, it appears red in color. However, this is just an illusion. The light from the sun appears colorless but is in fact made of different wavelengths. These wavelengths consist of light from different spectrums: Violet, green, blue, yellow, orange, and red. The rose is actually colorless. When sunlight shines on the rose, all of the light spectrums are absorbed by it, except the color red. It is this color that is reflected off the rose and is detected by your eyes, giving the rose the appearance of being red. But the illusion of color is just the beginning of the mind's illusion.

The rose that you look at is actually found within your mind, rather than in the garden. When you look at the rose or any object for that matter, your eyes are taking in information. This information is collected by the retina of your eye and then converted into electrical impulses by the optic nerve. The optic nerve transmits the electrical impulses to the brain, which then creates a conceptual image of the rosebush. Your other senses, such as touch and smell, process information the same way. This information is also transmitted to the brain as electrical impulses. The brain then converts this information and adds it to the image that it created. In truth, all of our experiences are a projection of the mind. As we see ourselves as being separate beings, we interpret these projections as a being a physical world that exists independent of ourselves.

Emotions

Our emotions are equivalent to a car's GPS device as they provide insight as to whether we are traveling in the right direction, which is home. What is your home? Your home is becoming aligned with your essential and non-physical self, which is pure consciousness. We are multidimensional beings whose essential self is consciousness while simultaneously manifesting as a mind and physical body.

Earlier it was explained that deep sleep shares the same qualities of pure consciousness, which includes the lack of thought or experience. For consciousness to expand, it needs information, which comes in the form of experiences. It is for the purpose of experiencing that our essential self-manifests as our physical self; it requires a mind and physical body to have an experience. Having a mind and a physical body creates the belief that we are individual and autonomous beings, which is necessary for creating a sense of separation from the world around us. It is this sense of separation that creates experience, which leads to the expansion of both you as pure consciousness as well as a manifested being.

Your emotions are the universe's way of informing you as to whether or not you are aligned with your essential self. When we are aligned with our essential aspect, we experience what we have come to call "positive emotions." When we lose our alignment with our essential aspect, we then experience "negative emotions." Anytime you are feeling a sense of love, appreciation, gratitude, compassion, happiness, or forgiveness, you are in alignment. Anytime that you are feeling fear, anxiety, anger, envy, jealousy, greed, or a sense of lack, you are out of alignment.

Emotions create a continuum from low frequency to high frequency. At the low end of the continuum is the emotion of helplessness. When we experience this emotion, we feel like victims and feel powerless to change our situation. Emotions associated with helplessness are despair, grief, sadness, and regret. Higher on the lower end of the scale is fear. Fear is a higher frequency than the emotion of helplessness because fear can lead to taking action. The emotion of anger is a higher frequency than fear as anger is more action oriented. Above anger are emotions such as worry, doubt, and disappointment. In the middle of the continuum are emotions such as contentment, and hopefulness. Further up the scale are emotions such as enthusiasm and optimism. Moving toward the high end are the emotions of gratitude, joy, and empowerment. The highest level frequencies are that of appreciation and love.

The emotion of appreciation is of the same frequency as love, which is fortunate for us. Many of us find appreciation an easier emotion to cultivate than love, especially the love of self. Before we go any further, it is important to point out that gratitude, which is a positive emotion, is of a lower frequency than appreciation, making it a less effective emotion for manifesting. The reason for that is the emotion of gratitude is conditional, while appreciation is non-conditional. We are normally grateful for having received something. I may be grateful for my friends because of what I get from having them in my life. I may be grateful for my health because of what health allows me to do with my life. Appreciation is non-conditional in that I can appreciate something without gaining anything from it. I can appreciate the goodness of other people for how they help others. I can appreciate a beautiful sunset for its sheer beauty, and I can appreciate the dedication that an artist or craftsperson gives to their creation.

Our emotions mirror our thoughts. We may not always be aware of our thoughts, especially those that are subconscious; however, we will know of their presence within us by the emotions that we experience. If you have negative emotions, then at some level of your being, you are having negative thoughts. Conversely, if you have positive emotions, you are experiencing positive thoughts. By understanding that our emotions are both a mirror of our thoughts and a GPS to our essential self, we can use them to become conscious creators through the Law of Attraction. The key to becoming a conscious creator is to be aware of both our emotions and our intent.

The following is a review as to what has been discussed so far:

1. We are multidimensional beings, whose essential nature is non-physical, non-local, and pure awareness while simultaneously appearing as a physical being.
2. At our most essential nature, there is only oneness, without any sense of separation or distinction. At our manifested level, we experience separation. Experiencing separateness allows to us to experience contrast.
3. The experience of contrast serves our expansion at the manifest level and at our essential level, which is consciousness.
4. Our emotions are the equivalent of a GPS that informs us to the alignment of our manifested being with our non-physical self.
5. Awareness of our emotions and our intent allows us becoming conscious creators.

The Power of Emotions to Attract

As previously stated, everything that exists is composed of energy and that energy can take on the form of different wavelengths or frequencies. Whenever two things share the same frequency, they will be attracted to each other. Similarly, when two things have different frequencies, they will repel each other. Our thoughts will attract into our lives those things that are of the same frequency. Most of us have difficulty in discerning the quality of the thoughts that we are thinking due to a lack of awareness, especially at the sub-conscious level. That which enables us to overcome this challenge is our emotions; our emotions are an indicator of the kind of thoughts that we are thinking; hence, they inform us to the frequency that we are at any given moment. By raising our emotions, we can raise our frequency. To become a conscious manifester, we need to understand our patterns of thoughts at both the subconscious and conscious level. Being emotionally aware makes this possible.

Our challenge is that most of us gave up control of our emotions at an early age. We have learned to attribute the emotions that we experience to conditions outside ourselves. We have been conditioned to believe that other people, events, situations, or our circumstances, create our emotional experience. Thus, to change our emotions, we need to change the world around us.

As the essence of who we are is energy and consciousness, our emotions are created by us. There is nothing that you can experience that can make you feel a certain way. Rather, we project our emotions on our experience and then believe that it is our experience that is making us feel the way we do. An example would be that you are driving and the driver in the next lane cuts you off while merging into your lane. You may feel that the other driver caused you to feel angry when in a fact anger is part of your make-up; the other driver was just a stimulus that elicited the arising of anger from within you. If anger was truly caused by the other driver, then every driver who ever got cut off would get angry, which is not the case. Based on this scenario, you projected anger on your experience of the other driver.

By believing that other people, circumstances, and events are the cause for how we feel, we have surrendered our power as spiritual beings and allowed our environment to dictate how we feel. This surrendering of power, along with our socialization, leads us to believe in scarcity of those resources that we believe we need to be happy. How we were raised, our culture beliefs, advertisers, politics, and even religion, often prey on our subconscious fears of scarcity. The fear of scarcity leads us to base our sense of identity and self-worth on how well we meet the societal image of success. When we feel that we do not measure up to these artificial standards for success, we often cope in ways that become habitual patterns for us. As these patterns become so ingrained in us, we are unconscious of them, and they become part of our self-image. Examples of such patterns include arrogance, greed, mistrust, envy, being competitive, risk-taking behaviors, attention seeking behaviors, addictive behaviors, low self-esteem, being introverted, and being extroverted. We incorporate these patterns into our self-image to avoid feeling less about ourselves for not meeting the expectations that we bought into.

For example, an arrogant person and a person who has low self-esteem both are suffering from the belief that they do not meet the expectations of others. The only difference between these two people is how they have dealt with the fear of being inadequate. The arrogant person has adopted the belief that they are better than others, while the person with low self-esteem has adopted the persona that prevents them from challenging themselves and possibly failing. At some level of our being, each one of us holds onto a false image of ourselves that we believe will protect us from being seen as not being good enough.

The lies we tell ourselves, the fears that we are hiding from, and the hopes and dreams that we have for our future, are all being transmitted to the larger consciousness, also known as the universe. The frequencies that we transmit to the universe will return to us in like kind. In this manner, we are like the person who goes to the magical restaurant who is unclear as to what to order. Just like this patron, that which we hope for, that which we do not care about, and that which grosses us out will be served to us. In the following chapters, we will discuss how to be as the first patron of the magical restaurant and get that which you really want.

The Law of Attraction Mindset

The quality of your thoughts and emotions will attract into your life that which is of like quality. The main reason why people get disappointing results with the Law of Attraction is due to a lack of awareness of subconscious beliefs. Subconscious beliefs generate a frequency that becomes a counter force when attracting that which is desired. A person may have a conscious desire to attract more money but subconsciously have the belief that they are not deserving or that their situation will never change. Since we are unaware of our subconscious beliefs, they have a greater power than our conscious beliefs. To expose our subconscious beliefs, we need to give up our resistance to them as it is our resistance that makes them subconscious. Going back to the example of the person who wants to attract money, it is their subconscious belief that they are not deserving that will attract those conditions that are a match to that belief. Instead of attracting more money, they will attract situations and events that create financial struggles.

The Law of Attraction mindset is that of non-resistance. The Law of Attraction operates based on our focus and intent. Which we are resistant to will receive the lion's share of our focus. Fortunately, there are exercises that we can do to reduce our resistance and unveil our subconscious beliefs, or feelings so that we can regain alignment with our essential self.

Chapter 2
How to Remove Resistance

Increasing our frequency requires the removal of resistance, and the removal of resistance requires raising awareness of the beliefs that are limiting us. There are two major ways for removing resistance, with the first way being the cultivation of love and appreciation. The second way is increasing your awareness to the mental phenomena of your mind.

Love and Appreciation

The frequent references to love as being the most powerful force in the universe, or that love conquers all goes beyond being poetic or spiritual speak; it is a reality! The power of love is that it melts resistance. When we experience love for anything, we give up any sense of resistance toward ourselves or that which we experience love for. To experience love is to experience oneness with our beloved. Because love removes resistance, all blockages are removed from the manifestation process. The challenge for many of us is our ability to cultivate a sense of love, especially a love for ourselves. Self-love is the ultimate spiritual achievement as it is the optimal state for manifestation as well as providing others an opportunity to catch a glimpse of their own divinity.

In many ways, self-love is the equivalent of enlightenment, for to achieve self-love is to cause the darker aspects of our nature to lose their power, which releases a tremendous amount of energy that can be used in the manifestation process. When we reach self-love, the Law of Attraction takes on a paradoxical place in our lives. When we have self-love, we become masters of manifesting due to the lack of resistance. However, since we experience self-love, there is little need to manifest anything given that there is no longer a sense of wanting. Self-love makes us feel complete or whole. It is for this reason that the learning of how to effectively use the Law of Attraction should be viewed as being less than a way to get what we desire and more as a stepping stone to learning the truth of who we are. In this manner, the Law of Attraction is ultimately a practice of self-discovery.

Self-Love

One of the challenges of developing self-love is that we associate self-love with selfishness or narcissisms; however, there is a big difference between self-love, selfishness, and narcissism.

Selfishness arises from a belief system that is fear based. People who are selfish do not feel in control of their lives and see the world through the lens of scarcity. For them, there is not enough love, money, or resources to go around. Because they feel that they are not in control of their lives, and there is only a limited amount of resources available, everyone around them is viewed as a competitor. To give anything up to another is seen as a threat to getting their needs met.

While the selfish person feels that their life is out of control, the narcissist has a belief system that leads to a sense of grandiosity. Narcissistic people are unable to empathize with others and have a need for admiration.

Self-Love is the polar opposite of selfishness and narcissism. Self-love is based on the understanding that each one of us is intimately connected to the universe and that we are interdependent upon each other. It is in our own personal expansion that we become a mirror to others for their own expansion; however, our own personal expansion can only come from honoring ourselves. Self-love is like the lighting of one candle so that it can be used to light all the other candles on a menorah. The following are comments and exercises on generating self-love and appreciation.

Values

When cultivating self-love, it is essential that we learned to live by our values. Anytime we live in a manner that is inconsistent with our values, we create major resistance in our lives. If your life is not aligned with your values, start the process of making changes in your life so that you can start creating greater alignment. If you currently have a job that conflicts with your values, what can you do to create the needed changes in your work? Could you conduct your work differently? Would it require you take on a different position? Perhaps it means finding a new job. If the relationship you are in does not align with your values, what changes do you need to make? Do you need to transform your relationship or find a new one? Take into account any aspect of your life where you experience a gap between the way you live your life and the values that you hold.

Whose Life is it?

To be a successful manifester requires personal integrity. While your emotions are a mirror to your thoughts, your feelings are your connection to universal intelligence. Though your emotions are a GPS to the larger consciousness, they still are based on thoughts, which can rapidly change. Given that our feelings are directly connected with universal intelligence, they are more accurate than our emotions. Anytime we compromise how we feel to meet the expectations of others, we lose our alignment. To honor our feelings is one of the greatest practices of self-love. Your feelings are your own unique GPS; no one else has the same GPS as you do. The greatest gift you can give to those that you love and care about is to become a living example of self-love, so that they can learn to love themselves. The following exercise will help you expand your awareness of honoring your feelings.

Go into meditation and make the intention that you will develop the awareness to catch yourself when you go against your feelings. As you go through your day, take notice whenever you go against the way you feel. Anytime you experience feelings of uneasiness, it is a sign that you are thinking thoughts or taking actions that go contrary to your feelings. Examples include:

- Agreeing to join others in an activity when you really would prefer to be alone.
- Feeling that you want to do something but rationalizing that you have more important things to do.
- Feeling like that you want just to relax and do nothing, while telling yourself that doing so would be irresponsible.
- Following the lead of others even though you do not feel right about it, an example of which would be peer pressure.
- Doing things always the same way just because you were taught or raised to believe that it is the way that it should be done.

After completing this exercise, schedule a day that you can devote to yourself. During this day, you are only going to do only those things that are consistent with how you feel. Most people have difficulty with this exercise as it goes against how we were raised. If this is the case, you may want to commit to a few hours instead of a whole day. As you feel more comfortable with this exercise, extend the time frame until you can dedicate the whole day to it.

Another challenge people experience with this exercise is that there are things they do not want to do, but they have to do it. This exercise is not about avoiding reality or daily responsibilities; rather, it is about learning to change our perspective. If you encounter a situation where you do not feel like doing something, but it has to be done, do one of the following:

1. Think about the benefits of doing the task and the consequences of not doing it. If the benefits of completing the tasks outweigh the consequences of not doing it, you should feel less resistance doing the task.
2. Think of how you could change your approach to doing the tasks in a manner that makes doing it more enjoyable. Example: If you need to do your taxes, put on your favorite music or invite a friend over so that you can do your taxes together.
3. If none of the previous suggestions change the way you feel about the task, postpone doing the task until you come to point where you can do it with acceptance.

The principle behind the last three suggestions is the eliminating of resistance. In fact, these suggestions having nothing to do with the task; rather, they are ways to modify your perception of it. The key to learning to cultivate self-love, and becoming a conscious manifester, is to learn how to modify your perceptions in a way that you no longer struggle against yourself. Self-love involves living your life based on the way you want to live it, rather than living according to the expectations or judgments of others.

Appreciation

As indicated earlier, many people have trouble experiencing self-love, so cultivating appreciation is an effective way of overcoming this obstacle while gaining the same results. To cultivate appreciation, do the following exercises as sequenced below:

A final important note: It is important to trust whatever responses you get when asking these questions. Trust the first answer that comes to you; do not worry about giving a wrong answer.

Exercise 1:

Think of someone or something that you love. As you think of your subject, think of all the ways that you appreciate them. Allow yourself to fully experience your feelings. Experience the love, joy, or other energies that arise. Feel these energies in your body. As you experience these energies, intensify their feeling by employing your other senses, such as touch, hearing, smelling, and taste. To do this, add these other sensory dimensions to your mind's representation of your subject. Example: If I am thinking of my spouse, I would not just imagine my spouse, I would also imagine his touch, hear his voice, the smell of his cologne, and the taste of his kiss. By engaging your other senses, the feelings of appreciation will become more deeply etched in your memory.

Exercise 2:

For this exercise, you are going to focus on a person or thing that you have neutral feelings for. For example, it could be the person at the register where you do your shopping, of whom you have no interest in. It could also be an object like a tree or a piece of furniture that you have no interest in. Think about what you can appreciate about your subject. As before, allow yourself to fully experience the feelings and attempt to intensify them by using your other senses.

Exercise 3:

This exercise involves you selecting a subject that annoys or irritates you at a moderate level. Think of that person that aggravates you or the animal or object that frustrates you. Focus on the behaviors or qualities that your subject possesses that you can appreciate. As in the previous exercises, allow yourself to fully experience the feelings and try to intensify them.

Exercise 4:

When you have been successful in the previous exercises, you are ready to perform this one. This exercise is to be conducted as you engage in your daily activities. Every opportunity you have, take the time to find something that you can appreciate. As with the previous exercises, allow yourself to fully experience the feelings and try to intensify them.

Optional: Exercise 5:

When you feel you have been successful in completing Exercise 4, you are ready for the real test. Think of someone who you hate. Try to find something about them that you can appreciate. Your appreciation has less to do with them and more with taking charge of your own energy level. By being able to generate appreciation for any quality that this person has, you can clear your resistance.

Meditation

The purpose of meditation is to redirect your attention from the outer world and redirect it toward your inner world. Your outer world is a reflection or projection of your inner world; only when you understand your inner world can you move beyond the illusions of your mind. When you can get clarity of your inner world, you will be better prepared to use the Law of

Attraction with greater precision. Meditation allows us to bring the power of awareness to all mental phenomena, including those that we are resisting. The power of awareness alone allows us to experience our mind a way that is harmonious, rather than adversarial.

There are some key points to keep in mind when learning how to meditate:

1. Maintain an attitude of total acceptance and non-judgment for everything you experience.
2. Do not try to control, change, or resist anything that you experience.
3. Allow all that you experience complete freedom to express itself.
4. When meditating, you may experience thoughts such as:
    a. My thoughts keep coming; they are not slowing down.
    b. This is too difficult.
    c. This is boring.
    d. I have more important things to do.
    e. This is not working.
    f. Am I doing this right?

Ignore these thoughts and continue to focus on the meditation.

Finally, there is no correct way or incorrect way to meditate as long as you are allowing yourself to be a witness to all of your experiences. No thought or experience can affect you as long as you do not provide it with your attention. It is your attention to the phenomena within your mind that give them their power. No thought or sensation inherently possesses its own power; their power is derived from your attention. Make a shift from giving thoughts your attention to simply being a silent witness to them.

1. Sit down in a comfortable position, close your eyes, and breathe normally.
2. Place your attention on your breath by focusing on the sensations of it traveling in and out of your body.
3. As your focus on your breath, you will experience the appearance of thoughts. When they appear, simply ignore them and return your attention back to your breath.
4. If you keep your focus on your breath, there will come the point when you can maintain your awareness of it without any effort. When you reach this stage, allow yourself to be the witness to all that appears in your awareness.
5. Notice how thoughts, sensations, and perceptions appear in your awareness and then fade away. These mental phenomena appear and disappear in your

awareness; yet, you as the observer of them remain constant.
6. The mental phenomena you experience will have the qualities of being positive, neutral, or negative as to how they make you feel, yet awareness itself is untouched by any of these qualities.
7. As you give less importance to the experiencing of mental phenomena, they will lose their energy, and your mind will become calm; you may even experience periods of stillness and space. If you do, know that this too is a kind of mental phenomena. Do not become attached to this experience; rather, remain as a witness to it as well. It too will come and go; this is okay. Just enjoy the experience while it lasts. It too will return to your awareness when the conditions are right.
8. The experiencing of stillness and space indicates that you have given up your attachments to mental phenomena; hence, you have given up your resistance to them as well. It is the fertile ground for manifesting. Release your intentions and then forget about them.
9. Continue to meditate for as long as you desire.

By practicing this meditation on a regular basis, you will discover that your discernment of mental phenomena will become greater as will your ability to remain still and silently observe them. The significance of this is that you will gradually lose your sense of resistance to these phenomena. Because of this, they will lose their strength to compete with your conscious mind when trying to attract that which you desire.

By not becoming attached to your intentions, you will not engage in doubt when their manifestation does not correspond to your expectations. It is our expectations of how and when our manifestations should appear that leads to doubt, thus the creation of resistance. Learn to release your intentions and then forget about them, just go on with your daily life.

Emotional Diving

Another technique to reduce resistance to your subconscious thoughts and feelings is to immerse yourself in them as opposed to keeping them suppressed. To do this exercise, do the following:

1. Think of a current thought that you have which is bothering you. For example: "I do not know if I can make my bills this month."
2. I would then ask myself: "How does that feel?" My response to the previous example would be: "I feel worried."

The remaining steps of this exercise require you to focus only on feelings that you experience, rather than thinking about it. For this reason, you want to repeatedly phrase your questions "How does that feel?" Each time you come up with a response, you are going to drill down deeper by repeating this question.

3. Continuing with my example, I would ask myself "How does being worried feel?" I would then focus on the sensations in my body, becoming completely immersed in them. My response might be: "Being worried makes me feel constricted and heavy."
4. I would then continue with the questioning by asking: "How does being constricted and heavy feel?" I would then immerse myself in the feelings of constriction and heaviness until a response came to mind, such as: "Feeling constricted and heavy feels like a huge weight is on me."
5. I would continue to drill down on my response by asking myself: "How does a huge weight feel?" I would then again immerse myself in the feelings until I got a response, such as: "It feels like I am being dragged to the ground."
6. I would continue my questioning until I started experiencing neutral or positive feelings.
7. When you reach this point, you have transformed your negative emotions.

This exercise allows you to transform your feelings until they are no longer attracting negativity into your life.

Loving Yourself

The following exercise is the one that people often find to be the most difficult. Due to our conditioning, most of us have learned to believe that we are unlovable or somehow flawed. This belief comes from the result that we have been socialized to believe that our self-worth is dependent upon the approval of others. The following exercise will allow you to recondition yourself to experience love for yourself. The one who can release resistance toward themselves is the one who can manifest without effort.

1. While before a mirror, look deeply into your eyes and tell yourself out loud "I love you" using your name.
2. Attempt to feel love for yourself. If you can experience the feelings of love, allow yourself to experience them as fully as possible. If you are unable to experience feelings of love, do not force it. Simply remain aware of any feelings that should arise without judgment.
3. Continue to look into your eyes, as you repeating say "I love you" to yourself by name. As you address yourself in this manner, place your focus on any emotions of appreciation, approval, or gratitude that you may experience.
4. You can tap into these emotions if you recall things that you have done that you feel good about. Incorporate all these memories in the way that you address yourself,

for example: "I love you (include your name) for the way you did…"
5. Focus on the feelings of love or appreciation that you experience as you do this exercise, while trying to intensify the feelings.
6. Try to do this exercise every morning and evening, allowing five minutes per exercise. Do this exercise daily until you begin to experience feelings of love or appreciation for yourself.

The following are additional methods for overcoming resistance:

Journaling

There is a power in writing that allows us to access the subconscious. It is why poets, musicians, and writers can express themselves more fully than if they just think about it. Most writers will tell you that, when they write, they are not the ones that are coming up with the ideas. Rather, they see themselves as being an instrument that is channeling some greater intelligence. Learn to journal daily, writing down whatever comes to mind. Continue writing until you feel satisfied emotionally.

Visualizations

Visualizing is great for accessing and influencing the subconscious; however, there are aspects of the visualizing process that are often misunderstood. The following are some key points to consider when visualizing:

1. There is an abundance of visualizing programs available on the market, and they can be useful if you have never visualized before. However, the most effective visualizations occur when you create your own visualizations. Once you understand the process, learn to trust your imagination and just go with it.
2. Many people feel they are unable to visualize, as they are unable to develop clear images in their mind. Do not worry about the quality of your images. However you experience your visualizations, trust them. Some people are unable to see images; rather, they experience sensations. With continued practice, your visualizations will become more vivid.
3. Before visualizing, it's helpful to formulate an intention for yourself. Examples of intentions would be:
    a. Visualizing your desires already manifested
    b. Visualizing yourself exploring that which you are resisting.
    c. Visualizing yourself taking on a new challenge as a form of a mental rehearsal.
    d. Visualizing yourself solving a problem.

Affirmations

Affirmations can be useful when manifesting; however, they need to be emotionally based to be effective. The mistake most people make when using affirmations is that they simply repeat the affirmation to themselves, which has little power. To be effective affirmations need to be accompanied by the generation of emotional intensity. As previously stated, emotions reflect your life state.

The exercises that we have just discussed in this chapter are based on conditioning. By associating the emotions of appreciation, love, or acceptance with our mental state, we can experience these emotions simply by entering the state. When this occurs, we do not have to meditate, visualize, or focus on appreciation. Just by entering the proper state, these emotions will arise in us automatically. What is the state that I speak of? It's the state that you experience when you make the decision to meditate or do any of these exercises. To do this, you first need to make these exercises part of your daily routine. With time, meditation or these exercises will become a habit for you. It is then that the simple thought of engaging in these activities will lead to experience the powerful emotions discussed in this chapter.

Chapter 3
Combining the Power of Emotion and Intention

Think of how a cell phone receives a signal from a transmitter. The transmitter is the metaphor for the source from which all things arise from, commonly referred to as universal consciousness, the higher self, the universe, or the quantum field. The strength of a cell phone signal will determine how clearly you can hear the other person as well as how clearly they can hear you. The Law of Attraction works the same way, the strength of your signal to the universe, as well as your ability to receive its signal, is dependent upon intention and emotion. Your intentions and emotions are the signals that connect you to the part of you that is universal and timeless. We will now discuss how these two components comprise the signal that is behind all of creation.

Intention

The intentions behind your desires are critical in the process of attraction as your intentions determine if you are broadcasting from the ego or love. As stated earlier, love has the highest frequency while fear has the lowest. It was also previously stated that we attract into our life that which matches our life's frequency. Whenever our intentions for attracting something into your life is based on self-interest, we have automatically weakened our signal. The reason for this is that intentions of self-interest are fear based. Conversely, when our intentions are for the wellbeing of others, our frequency operates from the level of love. Since love is the higher frequency, we will be more likely to attract that which we desire. For example, my intention may be to attract more money into my life. If my intention is due to the belief that I am inadequate as a person, because of money, I will be operating from fear. Fear will be the dominant frequency, and it will attract the people and situations that reinforce that perspective.

If on the other hand, my intentions are to attract money because doing so would allow me to take care of my family, or relieve the burden of another, then that intention comes from the place of love. As love has the highest frequency, the probability of me attracting it greatly increases.

Emotions

As previously mentioned, your emotions are a mirror to your dominant thoughts, both at the conscious and unconscious level. Rather than focusing on your thoughts to attract your desires, focus on the emotions that you associate with that which you are trying to attract. The best way to do this is through meditation. When your mind is calm, focus on what it would feel like if your desire was already manifested in your life. Allow yourself to feel the emotions and intensify the feelings you experience by thinking about all the benefits you would receive if your desires were manifested at this moment. Meditate at least twice a day, each time recreating these emotions by imagining that your desires were already manifested. Your meditation sessions should be only as long as you find them enjoyable. Continue your meditation until that which you desire manifests.

How Your Intentions Affect Consciousness

How intentions affect reality can be understood by using the metaphor of a video game. When playing a video game, you have an avatar that navigates its world. When engineers designed the game, they thought of every potential situation that your avatar could encounter and programmed it into the game. The potential situation that shows up in the game is determined by the actions that your avatar takes. The larger consciousness is like the engineer, while your physical manifestation is like the avatar. Your intentions affect the probability that potential situations will manifest in your life. Unlike the video game, which is limited in the potential responses that can be programmed into it, the larger consciousness expresses itself as infinite potential. The potential that expresses itself is determined by probability, but your intentions can affect the probability. The effect of intention on probability can be illustrated by using the example of traffic accidents. The universe holds a certain probability that traffic accidents will occur. However, this probability can be increased or decreased by the intentions held by the individual driver. If a driver is worried about getting in an accident, then that intention will increase the probability of an accident occurring. The reason for this is the driver is focusing on his or her fear of having an accident. If this same driver felt relaxed, was enjoying the drive, and was driving defensively, then the probability of being involved in an accident would drop.

The affecting of the probability for a potential to manifest can also be exemplified by the personality types of the optimist and pessimist. The reason why these personality types experience reality differently is that their dominant mindset affects the probability of whether they are presented with encouraging circumstances or discouraging circumstances. Because of their attitude, the optimist affects the probability of the universe in a way that causes the ratio of encouraging circumstances to be greater than the negative circumstances, while the pessimist attracts a ratio that is the opposite of the optimist.

Chapter 4
Putting the Pieces Together

So far we have covered a lot of information, so in this chapter we will put it all together to provide context, so that you can see how all these pieces fit together. As previously indicated, you are simultaneously pure consciousness at your most essential level and a physical being at the manifested level. What we commonly refer to as the universe is pure consciousness.

It is the nature of consciousness to expand. However, expansion requires new information, which is why consciousness manifests as phenomena. It is only through physicality that experience can occur. This is our purpose for being here, to experience. Experience is the result of contrast, which is why we manifested as a physical body. Having a physical body creates a sense of separation, resulting in the experience of contrast. Me and you, us and them, light and dark, hot and cold, peace and war, love and hate, affluence and scarcity, good and bad, all of these things are examples of contrast.

Contrast is the way we gain new information. This information is transmitted, as our intentions, back to our essential self, or the universe. It is the nature of the universe to answer all of our intentions, so it manifests the people, objects, situations, events, and circumstances that fulfill our intentions, which leads to new experiences. Our intentions provide the universe with new information for its expansion, while our experience leads to the expansion of our manifested self. This feedback loop is the basis for the Law of Attraction; the Law of Attraction is the ongoing communication between your manifested self and your non-physical self.

When you have an intimate understanding of the dynamics of the Law of Attraction, as just described, you will feel yourself become liberated. You will begin to understand that it is impossible to make a mistake in life, that everything you will ever experience is resulting in your expansion and that is the purpose of the universe to support you.

Chapter 5
The Law of Attraction and Relationships

Relationships are the most powerful tool for learning how to raise your vibration and becoming more self-aware. The people who have entered your life did so because you attracted them; there are no accidents or mistakes in this universe. Just as a magnet draws iron filings, you have drawn people toward you; your relationships are the mirror that allows you to view your subconscious. It is for this reason why we often hear of the story of the person who leaves a relationship because they are unhappy, only find themselves in the same situation upon entering a new relationship. Until we learn to use our relationships as a mirror to view the shadows within ourselves, we will continue to attract experiences that align with our darker side.

Before exploring more fully the dynamics of how relationships serve as a mirror, it is important to repeat a statement that was made earlier in this book, which is that all of our experiences are the projections of our own mind. Your relationships, as is will all of life, are a mirror of your inner world. However, as long as we base our experience of life on intellectual or rational thinking, we will attribute our problems to the people, situations, circumstances, and events "outside" ourselves.

As a child, Jane always felt that her father did not love her. Unlike her siblings, who he seemed to enjoy being with, he seemed distant to her. Further, she was always a child who was naturally curious and wanted to explore the world around her. Her parents, who came from a traditional upbringing, would try to suppress her curiosity, believing that little girls should be quiet and reserved.

From the time we were infants, we learn that we need to depend on our parents to get our needs met. If we won our parent's approval, we were more likely get what we wanted. If we did not meet their expectations, it might have led to punishment or disapproval. To meet the expectations of our parents, we had to suppress some of our natural qualities that were disapproved of while adopting new beliefs or behaviors that met our parent's expectations. Jane learned that being curious and explorative was not rewarded while being quiet and reserved was. Further, she developed the belief that the reason for her father being distant was because she was unlovable.

Through continued exposure to her parents, Jane learned to suppress her desire for curiosity and exploration until they became part of her subconscious; these qualities become unrecognizable to her. She came to see herself as being quiet and reserved. She also became judgmental or critical of those people who she saw as being curious and adventurous, especially those who were strong in these traits. She felt this way toward them because, at a subconscious level, they reminded her of the pain that she experienced for being that way herself. As for her relationship with her father, she subconsciously attracted men into her life who were also distant with her.

Jane's story is our story as we all have learned to suppress natural aspects of who we are to be accepted. Though we may not be conscious of these suppressed aspects, they attract the people and situations into our lives that are consistent with their frequency. It is for this reason that many people have problems getting the result they want from life; they are unaware of the fact that they are broadcasting a signal to the universe that contradicts that which they consciously desire. Remember, the Law of Attraction is always working, whether we believe in it or not. The only question is: are we aware of what we are broadcasting to the universe, both consciously and unconsciously?

No thought or emotion is inherently negative or positive. It is us that assign meaning to our thoughts and emotions. All of our sufferings and unhappiness are the result of us judging our thoughts and emotions and developing resistance toward them. When we can give up our resistance toward any aspects of ourselves, we free up energy and quiet the mental noise that absorbs our focus. From the perspective of higher awareness, there is nothing in this universe that is inherently good or bad. Even those aspects of ourselves that we attempt to suppress or battle with have noble aspects about them, aspects that serve us. When we give up our resistance to anything in life, it will work on our behalf.

Befriending Your Unconscious Aspects

The following is an exercise that you can use in any of your relationships for healing those unconscious aspects of yourself that are holding you back from improving your life.

1. Think of a person in your life who has a quality about them that bothers you.
2. When you have identified that quality, write it down on a piece of paper. I recommend that you use one piece of paper for each quality that you identify.
3. For each quality, write out all the reasons why this quality bothers you. For example, if the offending quality of the other person is that they are insensitive, you could write something like this:
"By being insensitive, you make the world colder. It can lead to others feeling hurt, and it prevents you from experiencing the emotions and feelings of others. Being insensitive is like living in a barren desert".
4. Remember that how you experience the outer world around is a reflection of your inner world. That which bothers you in others is also found to some degree

within you as well. If you are disturbed by the insensitivity of others, it is because you have insensitivity within you, and you associate emotional pain to being insensitive.

5. Now reflect on the benefits of having that quality, though perhaps to a lesser degree than you perceive in the other person.
6. Going back to the previous example, a benefit of having a degree of insensitivity may be that you are not bothered by what other people think of you; it would make you less reactive emotionally. It would provide you with a greater degree of freedom by allowing you to do the things you want to do, without worrying about what other people might think.
7. By acknowledging the nobility of your subconscious aspects, you relinquish your resistance to it. In doing so, these aspects will lose their potency as a counterforce when you are consciously attracting that which you desire.

It is highly recommended that you practice this exercise with people with whom who you do not have an emotional connection. When you become more confident in this technique, start practicing it with those relationships with whom you have a strong emotional connection.

When you can truly experience this exercise, you will come to a revolutionary understanding, which is this: Every person that has ever entered your life did so because you attracted them. Not only did you attract them, but they also entered your life as a guide or mirror for your next expansion. For this reason, your search for Mr. or Ms. Right is just a fairy tale. In truth, every person who has ever entered your life was the perfect person for you at that time.

Our desire to find that perfect person arises from the belief that by doing so we will feel whole, that we are incomplete until then. In truth, your sense of wholeness can only come about when you can allow each person who enters your life to mirror back your projections, without blaming them or yourself. Use the exercise in this chapter to learn what the other person is revealing about you. At the level of higher awareness, the ideal relationship is not about making each other happy; it is about supporting each other as each person discovers their own truth and happiness.

Entering the Perspective of Another

Ultimately, the key to creating a fulfilling relationship lies in the ability to understand the perspective of another person and honoring it. This understanding leads us to a discussion of the Law of Attraction that is usually not elucidated. The Law of Attraction is often discussed from the perspective of attracting relationships, money, or other physical items into our lives;

however, a discussion of attracting insights is often absent. To better understand this, it is first necessary to develop an understanding of the nature of thought.

As indicated throughout this book, we identify with our minds and bodies, creating a sense that each one of us is a physical being that is separate from other living beings. This sense of separateness extends to the mental phenomena that we experience, which includes thought. We believe that our thoughts are created by us, that our thoughts are the exclusively from our own minds. Further, we experience our thoughts as being reality, which then leads to the creation of expectations. Now where are our expectations more evident than in our relationships.

All arguments and struggles within our relationships are the result of other people not meeting the expectations that we hold in our heads. If we are firmly attached to our thoughts and expectations, there can be no space or flexibility to accommodate alternate perspectives. With a deeper understanding of the nature of thought and the Law of Attraction, we can reveal our greater potential for creating extraordinary relationships.

As stated earlier, we are multidimensional beings who are both non-physical and physical simultaneously, with our essential nature being pure consciousness. Pure consciousness is the source of all physical reality, including thoughts. Physical reality is created by consciousness expressing itself at a lower frequency, thus becoming phenomenal. The term phenomenal refers to anything that can be detected by the mind, which is why thoughts are considered to be part of our physical reality.

As physical beings, we do not create our thoughts; rather, thoughts are the expressions of our nonphysical self and are picked-up by our physical self. Since there is one pure or universal consciousness, all of humanity has equal accesses to any thought that has ever or will ever be thought. The thoughts of Julius Caesar as those of future generations are all accessible through the larger consciousness. It is this nature of consciousness that the concept of the Akashic Records is based on. The Akashic Records are the holding place of information for all lives, past, present, and future. Information on the single lifetime of each person is kept as a record, just as there are different volumes in a series of books. Each record is a lifetime of thoughts for that person.

Your individual or personal consciousness is just a subset of the larger universal consciousness, just as a drop of water is a subset of the ocean. Just as an antenna picks up radio signals from a radio tower, your personal consciousness attracts thoughts from the universal consciousness. You attract those thoughts that are of the same frequency as your life state, which is determined by the existing beliefs that you hold. Universal consciousness is like an infinite buffet, and each one of us is selecting the menu items that matches our individual taste.

By learning to calm our minds through meditation, we can use the Law of Attraction to gain access to the perspective of the people that we have relationships with. All arguments and misunderstandings with other people are the result of not being able to move beyond our own perceptions, making it impossible for us to perceive the other person's perceptions. It just as a person who only speaks English trying to understand someone who only speaks Spanish. We can enter another person's perspective by holding the sincere intention to do so and then creating the space to receive this information.

The following is an exercise for doing so, though it is important to note that success in this technique requires practice, the ability to enter a meditative state, and the ability to remain open. Do the following:

1. Before entering your meditation, think about the person whose perspective you want to enter.
2. When thinking about this person, think of their frustrations and concerns that they have and the reasons for it. You do not have to understand or even agree with their perspective; your job is to just recognize their frustrations.
3. Announce to yourself your intention to enter this person's perspective.

4. Enter your meditation, reminding yourself again of your intention.
5. When you reach a calm mental state, repeat the intention one last time. From this point on, do not make any attempts to influence your experience or hold any expectations. Simply remain open and allow whatever you experience to present itself.
6. Practice by repeating this exercise until you experience the perceptive of the other person.

This next meditation can be used to manifest the relationship that you desire.

1. Sit down in a comfortable position, close your eyes, and breathe normally.
2. Place your attention on your breath by focusing on the sensations of it traveling in and out of your body.
3. As your focus on your breath, you will experience the appearance of thoughts. When they appear, simply ignore them and return your attention back to your breath.
4. If you keep your focus on your breath, there will come the point when you can maintain your awareness of it without any effort. When you reach this stage do the following:

a. Imagine how you would feel emotionally if you had the relationship that you desired? Experience these emotions as fully as possible.
b. Imagine what you would see if you had the relationship that you desired.
c. Imagine what you would touch if you had the relationship that you desired.
d. Imagine what you would hear if you had the relationship that you desired.
e. Make these experiences as real as possible and then intensify the feelings.

5. When you are ready, awake from your meditation.

Chapter 6
The Law of Attraction and Work

What is your purpose for working? Is it to earn money so that you can support yourself? Is it because it fulfills you? Is because you are passionate about your field of work. If you want to live from a higher level of awareness and make a greater difference by what you do, you may want to view work differently. Rather than just viewing work as a means to get money or a certain feeling, what if we viewed work as a means to express love?

As long as we view work solely for what we can get out it, we are operating from a place of scarcity. Your essential nature is that of absolute abundance and is devoid of need. In fact, you as your essential nature does not need to do anything as you are beyond need. What if we changed our purpose for working from gaining something to giving something? At the most basic level, all work involves providing a product or service to the customer. If I sell cars, I may have the belief that to be successful, I need to work hard and meet my quotas. Based on this model, I need to make a concerted effort in order to sell cars if I am to earn money. What if we adopted a new paradigm and identified our talents, skills, and passions and made love our service or product? Your talent and skills are love manifested in a way that is uniquely your own. What you do for work is just the context for expressing love, which is your true product or service.

Rose is a clerk at a busy convenience store; however, being a clerk is just a job title. Her real job is to give love to every customer that enters the store. Most customers who come into the store do so because of how Rose makes them feel, what they buy is only secondary. She is quick to greet them and ask them how they are doing. While most people who work at the store see it just as a job, Rose uses her position to give love. Because her focus is on creating love and value for her customers, Rose does not experience her job as "work." For her, the convenience store is her second home, and her customers are her family. Because of her attitude, she cannot help but positively impact her job, and management notices. She has received several promotions and enjoys the favor of her employer. Rose's love is expressed in everything she does in her job, and every person who is fortunate to come in contact with her is benefited in a way that is unique to them. Rose is the darling of her management team, and they support her any way that they can.

The most powerful force for attraction is love, and it is also the most powerful creative force. Those who love what they do may seem to work hard, but for them, it does not feel like it.

Whenever we do what we love, our actions seem to flow effortlessly, and we lose track of time. Not only do our actions flow effortlessly, but we also come up with our best ideas. What has just been described is the state of flow, or being in the zone. The state of flow comes when we allow our essential self to take precedence over our thinking. To be in the flow state is to be in love.

Most people think that we need to be doing a certain activity to be in flow. While it is true that flow state is most often achieved when we are doing things that we enjoy, this is just an illusion that we have come to believe. You are the creator of your experience, and you are the one that provides the meaning to experience. The activity or work that you are doing is just a prop. Everything you feel or think is projected onto experience; experience cannot make you feel anything. The difference between someone who loves their job and someone who hates their job has nothing to do with the job. The difference between these two people is what they are projecting onto the job. As long as we feel our experience is the determining factor of how we feel, we will live our life in a reactive manner toward our experience. When we come to realize that we create our experience and its meaning, then we have the power to get into the flow state and be love, regardless of the situation. Reaching this state of existence takes time, patience, and a committed practice of meditation or other contemplative practice.

Regardless of what your job is, whether you work for someone else or for yourself, ultimate success comes when your primary product or service is love, and you take ownership of it. It is not what you do but how you do it. When every aspect of our work life is based on love, you will be successful. How do you base your work or business on love? You treat what you do as if you owned it, and you expect only the highest quality from yourself. Everything you do you do as though it was a sacred act, a gift to your beloved. This type of attention needs to flow through every aspect of your work. It means becoming fully aware how you interact with your team members, your customers, your vendors, your processes, and your systems. Your focus needs to be how you can provide the greatest care in all that you do. True prosperity comes to those who create the greatest value for those they serve, and who you serve is all of life. The following are characteristics of love based work:

1. Taking a sense of ownership of all aspects of the workplace or organization.
2. Considering the organization's problems as your problem.
3. Constantly looking for ways to improve things and sharing them with the decision makers.
4. Conducting your work as though the final product or service is for your beloved.
5. Taking action to support others who are experiencing challenges in the workplace.

6. Extending your sense of responsibility from your assigned work to the organization as a whole.
7. Finding ways to improve the customer's experience.

If you have your own business and are self-employed, the characteristics of a love based business are:

1. Constantly looking for ways to improve your systems and processes.
2. Conducting your business as though the final product or service is for your beloved.
3. Treating your team members, your customers, and your vendors as your most important resource.
4. Finding ways to conduct business that minimizes the impact on the planet and is sustainable.
5. Eliminating processes that result in social injustice.

No work can be truly successful long term or create true value as long as the focus is just on making money. True success comes when our endeavors create lasting value for the planet as a whole. Some businesses are extremely successful by conventional standards; however, their success is just an illusion if there is no focus on the cost of doing business. Whether it is the destruction of the environment or the exploitation of people, eventually the costs to the world will not be able to be ignored. When we work through love, we will personally benefit as will the world. It will happen because we will be attracting into our life the very best that the universe can serve.

Exercise 1

1. Take time to reflect on the past and try to remember the times when you were the happiest. When you remember a specific time, think about what you were doing at the time as well as how you were doing it. For example, if you were happiest when you were creative, what was the context in which you were creative? Were you being creative for the benefit of another? Were you being creative just to express yourself? In your memory, were other people involved? Be sure to write down all of this information.
2. When you can get the details of the memory, repeat this exercise again by choosing another memory. Complete this process until you run out of memories.
3. Now think of your skills and talents. Make a list of all those things that you are good at. Your skills and talents should be those things that come naturally to you; you do them without any effort. Examples include:
    - Being compassionate
    - Being a good listener
    - Having a sense of humor
    - Being creative
    - Being good with numbers

- Computer skills
- Speaking skills
- Analytical abilities
- Athletic ability

When you have completed your list review them and allow yourself to experience the feelings that arise when you read your lists.

After you have reviewed your list, meditate. As you go deeper into your meditation, ask the universe for guidance on how you could use your talents and skills in a way that will create value and happiness for yourself and others. As you meditate, allow yourself to experience the feelings that you would have if you were already working in your dream job. Spend as much time as you can immersing yourself in that feeling. Continue this meditation each day until you receive the guidance that you need for manifesting your desire. When this happens, continue this meditation until your dream job is fully manifested.

Exercise 2

1. Sit down in a comfortable position, close your eyes, and breathe normally.
2. Place your attention on your breath by focusing on the sensations of it traveling in and out of your body.

3. As your focus on your breath, you will experience the appearance of thoughts. When they appear, simply ignore them and return your attention back to your breath.
4. If you keep your focus on your breath, there will come the point when you can maintain your awareness of it without any effort. When you reach this stage, think about how you would feel emotionally if you had the work that you desired? Experience these emotions as fully as possible.
5. Imagine what you would see if you had the work that you desired.
6. Imagine what you would touch if you had the work that you desired.
7. Imagine what you would hear if you had the work that you desired.
8. Make these experiences as real as possible, making them more intense whenever possible and then let them go.
9. When you are ready, awake from your meditation.

Chapter 7
The Law of Attraction and Money

Of all the areas in our lives, few affect us as profoundly as that of money. Whether it is an abundance of it or a lack of it, money can have a powerful emotional impact on us. Whether rich or poor, money plays a dominant role in the consciousness of most people. Because of this, we have developed strong beliefs and attitudes about money. Here are just a few examples of the more common ones:

- Money is the root of all evil.
- Money does not grow on trees
- The desire for money is not spiritual.
- Most rich people got that way by taking advantage of others.
- It is selfish to ask for things that we cannot afford.
- I cannot become financially successful because I have too many things stacked against me.
- It takes money to make money.

What all these beliefs point to is a misunderstanding of money as each of these beliefs imply that money has inherent power or value to it, that money causes us to behave in a certain way. Let us begin by debunking these beliefs and explore a more empowering perspective of money that can free us from the fetters that we have attached to both money and ourselves. Money is just a means to measure the exchange of value. If I pay a vendor $50 for a new pair of shoes, then both the vendor and I have agreed that the shoes are worth $50. The worth of money is purely subjective as our government assigns the value to money.

The value of money used to be based on the gold standard. As we are no longer on the gold standard, the value of money is purely subjective. What is not subjective is that which it purchases. The shoes that I purchased have inherent value, which was established by the vendor at $50. The value of the money that I used to purchase the shoes is subjective and can change during periods of inflation. The mistake many people make is that they focus on making money, which has no inherent value, instead of focusing on the value that they have to offer, which creates money. Money is made when we find a way to create value for others, and they are willing to compensate us for it.

Some people have generated millions of dollars and have lost it all, only to rebuild their wealth again. There are also people who can only dream of becoming rich and who live out their lives in scarcity. There is only one thing that separates these two groups and that is their beliefs.

The person who was born rich, or created their own fortune, have a mindset that provides them with a sense of certainty that they can attract money. For these people, making money just comes naturally. Those who have never experienced financial richness have developed a mindset of scarcity. That sense of scarcity is only reinforced by their family's history, the neighborhood that they live in, or the stereotypes that they have bought into through socialization.

If our dominant belief is that we can create wealth, then that is what will appear in our lives, given that we apply ourselves and find a way to create value for others. Conversely, if our belief is that we are impoverished, that we were born disadvantaged, that we cannot get a break, then that is what we will attract.

The difference between wealth and poverty has less to do with money and opportunity than it has to do with mindset. Henry Ford, Steve Jobs, Oprah Winfrey, J.K. Rowling, and Chris Gardner are just a few examples of people who came from very modest beginnings or even homelessness, only to generate fortunes as adults.

Regardless of what your story is, the formula for generating money is not as difficult as it may seem, especially when you consciously employ the Law of Attraction. The following sequence of exercises will point you in the right direction as it will address both your conscious and subconscious mind.

Exercise 1: Examine Your Beliefs about Money

Write out a list of all your beliefs about money. If needed refer to the examples in the earlier part of this chapter. When you write your list, do not make it an intellectual exercise. Instead, write whatever comes to mind.

When you have completed your list, review each belief. If the belief does not make you feel empowered, draw a line through it and create a new belief that both resonates with you and empowers you. Note: Refer to the exercise in Chapter 10, *Exercise for Changing a Belief* for instructions on how to install your new belief.

Example:

Old belief: Money does not grow on trees.

New belief: Money grows from the ideas that I foster and pursue.

Exercise 2: Know yourself

Money is created when we create value that fulfills a need. When the value that you provide also happens to align with your passion and joy, while filling a need, then you have a winning formula.

Take time to reflect on what you enjoy doing. Think about what makes you happy or passionate. If there is something that you enjoy doing, then odds are you are also good at it. Make a list of all the things that you can think of. They could be as simple as enjoying talking to being as complex as repairing computers.

Exercise 3: Identify your qualifications

Make a list of all your skills, talents, and knowledge base.

Skills are considered those abilities that you have that you had to learn. Examples:

- Accounting
- Repairing cars
- Scuba Diving

Talents are those abilities that come naturally to you; they did not require any learning. Examples:

- Being compassionate
- Having a sense of humor
- Being persuasive
- Being athletic

Knowledge based includes the knowledge that you gained from formal education, training, or from being self-taught.

Exercise 4: Identifying needs

This exercise involves identifying an unmet need. This need can be local, national, or global. Think of needs as problems, which can vary in magnitude. Problems can be as minor as forgetting where you left your keys or glasses to being as relevant as water conservation or energy shortages.

The last four exercises in this five step process serve the following purposes:

- Changing any disempowering beliefs about money can get you motivated.
- Creating financial success requires persistence and determination, which is why doing what you love will greatly improve your chances of success. If you love what you are doing, then you will more likely stick with it, despite the bumps in the road.
- Knowing your qualifications will provide a support structure for doing what you love.
- Identifying unmet needs will make what you have to offer relevant to others.

The last two exercises are for coming up with an idea and attracting money using the Law of Attraction.

Exercise 5: Coming up with a winning Idea and the Law of Attraction

Take time to reflect on the information that you gleaned from these exercises. Can you come up with an idea that fuses all these components together? Coming up with a winning idea can take time and research. If you find yourself unable to come up with an idea, you can also use the Law of Attraction.

The Law of Attraction can be used to find an idea and to attract the people and circumstances that can help you manifest a money making enterprise. It is important; however, to do the first three exercises before turning to the Law of Attraction. The information you gain from these exercises will clarify your intentions. To utilize the Law of Attraction, do the following:

1. Review your lists from the exercises in this chapter. You may also want to incorporate the lists from the chapter on work.
2. After reviewing the list, create an intention. Examples:
    a. I will find an idea that addresses a need and creates happiness for all involved.
    b. I will find a way to align my joys and strengths with service to others.
    c. I will attract the people and circumstances that will allow me to successfully serve others.

3. Enter your meditation. When you reach a calm state, release your intention. Upon releasing your intention, give up all attachment to it. Simply continue to live your life.
4. Repeat this meditation until you request is manifested.

Exercise 6: Attracting Money using the Law of Attraction

1. Sit down in a comfortable position, close your eyes, and breathe normally.
2. Place your attention on your breath by focusing on the sensations of it traveling in and out of your body.
3. As you focus on your breath, you will experience the appearance of thoughts. When they appear, simply ignore them and return your attention back to your breath.
4. If you keep your focus on your breath, there will come the point when you can maintain your awareness of it without any effort. When you reach this stage, think about how you would feel emotionally if you had the money that you desired? Experience these emotions as fully as possible.
5. Imagine what you would see if you had the money that you desired.
6. Imagine what you would touch if you had the money that you desired.

7. Imagine what you would hear if you had the money that you desired.
8. Make these experiences as real as possible, making them more intense whenever possible and then let them go.
9. When you are ready, awake from your meditation.

Chapter 8
The Law of Attraction and Health

As everything in this universe is made of energy, the Law of Attraction affects every aspect of our life, and our bodies are no exception. Our thoughts about our bodies and our health will manifest as our experience of them. From a universal perspective, both our bodies and health are the manifestation of thought. Our thoughts are so powerful that they can even override our genetics, which should be no surprise. While genetics may hold the blueprint of the body, that blueprint first had to be first created. What created the blueprint was consciousness. In fact, the power of consciousness over both our health and bodies can be witnessed in our daily lives.

While no one has come up with an accurate estimate, the number of cells in the human body can range from 50-70 trillion cells. Each one these cells are replaced after a period of days or months, depending on the cell. Further, each cell carries out numerous functions while coordinating its functions with all the other cells. What is it that orchestrates all this cellular activity seamlessly across the countless generations of cells?

As we go through the various stages of life, we undergo numerous changes. Our knowledge and understanding changes, our experience changes, and our bodies change. Despite all these changes, there is an aspect of us that is changeless. That which is changeless is our awareness. Regardless of all the transformations that we undergo, that which is aware of change remains unchanged. As consciousness, we are eternal and unchanging; however, our physical bodies are undergoing ongoing and continuous change by the second.

Why do some patients experience spontaneous remissions of cancer? Why does the placebo effect occur? How can it be that one person who takes a sugar pill, thinking that it is a new experimental drug, shows comparable therapeutic benefits as another patient who received actual medication? Why are well-respected scientists and medical groups funding research on the power of prayer on healing? All these questions continue to elude both scientist and researchers because they focus on the human body being as a mechanical and physical structure, rather than the expression of a unifying intelligence and wisdom, which is consciousness. The beliefs that we have regarding our health and bodies will materialize as our health and bodies.

When we express any resistance toward our bodies, the Law of Attraction will manifest in our bodies that which we focus on. If we fear that we are succumbing to illness, then that focus can manifest as real illness. If we focus on our dissatisfaction with our weight, our bodies will manifest the conditions that will make our weight loss attempts unsuccessful or non-sustainable.

If we focus on how we are getting older, the Law of Attraction will manifest those conditions that lead to the acceleration of the aging process.

If we focus on fear upon receiving a diagnosis of a life-threatening disease, our chance for survival will automatically be reduced. Similarly, if we focus on our desire to live our life fully, despite the diagnosis, our chances for recovery will be enhanced.

If we have a positive outlook toward life, feel love and appreciation for our lives, are forgiving toward ourselves and others, and pursue life with a sense of excitement, our mindset can negate the effects of unhealthy activities such as smoking. Most of us have heard the stories of how one individual engages in unhealthy activities and live a healthy long life, while another individual, who lives a life free of such activities, passes away early.

The guiding principle behind all the examples just described is that of emotion. Our emotional health determines the frequency of our bodies. High-frequency emotions will be reflected in the body's frequency, just as low-frequency emotions will reflect in the body. Self-love manifests as physical health, just as resistance toward ourselves manifest as health issues.

Where you are today with the health of your body is most likely due to your dominant beliefs. Our physiology is heavily influenced by our emotional health. An experiment was conducted where two subjects rode a roller coaster. Before riding the roller coaster, the subjects were tested to determine their physiological markers such as blood pressure, hormone levels, and other physiological factors. The first testing of the subjects was for establishing a baseline. The subjects then rode the roller coaster. The first subject loved the ride and could not wait to go back on. The second subject found the ride scary and could not wait for it to end. Upon the conclusion of the ride, the subjects were retested. The subject who enjoyed the ride had the physiological levels of a person experiencing wellbeing. The subject who found the ride to be a threatening experience expressed that in their physiology. Their stress hormones were elevated, while other physiological markers reflected a body that was experiencing stress. Both subjects experienced the same ride; the only difference was their beliefs about the experience.

Any time that we experience anything but sincere acceptance or love for our bodies, we are engaged in war with our bodies. Instead of trying to lose weight it would be more productive to focus on self-love and enjoying a healthy lifestyle.

Instead of trying to quit smoking, try living a life where every day you focus on experiencing greater meaning and fulfillment. Instead of succumbing to the belief that aging means a decline in your ability to enjoy life, start meditating to discover the truth of who you are, which is beyond beliefs. The aging process and the human lifespan that we have accepted to be fact are anything but that. Any aspect of the aging process is based on societal attitudes, statistics, and research, all of which are based on our limited human understanding. They are just a belief. Like the placebo effect, if we believe what society says, or what statistics and research reveal, our minds and bodies will comply.

As with any other aspect of life, we can base our lives on the mind, whose understandings are limited to concepts and intellect, or we can base our lives on the infinite potential of our greater consciousness. All that is required from us is to provide the intention; the universe will take care of everything else.

The health of our bodies is the physical expression of the health of our thoughts. Just as we should strive to remove resistance toward our mental phenomena, we would be wise to eliminate any resistance that we have for our bodies. Fortunately, by addressing our minds we will simultaneously address the body, and the most powerful way to do this is through cultivating self-love.

If you intend to use the Law of Attraction to improve your health, I urge you to do the self-love exercises described in Chapter 2, if you have not done them. When you have completed this exercise, advance to the following exercise.

Exercise

1. Sit down in a comfortable position, close your eyes, and breathe normally.
2. Place your attention on your breath by focusing on the sensations of it traveling in and out of your body.
3. As your focus on your breath, you will experience the appearance of thoughts. When they appear, simply ignore them and return your attention back to your breath.
4. If you keep your focus on your breath, there will come the point when you can maintain your awareness of it without any effort. When you reach this stage, think about how you would feel emotionally if you had the health that you desired? Experience these emotions as fully as possible.
5. Imagine what you would see if you had the health that you desired.
6. Imagine what you would touch if you had the health that you desired.
7. Imagine what you would hear if you had the health that you desired.

8. Make these experiences as real as possible, making them more intense whenever possible and then let them go.
9. When you are ready, awake from your meditation.

Chapter 9
Law of Attraction and Self-Improvement

We are a society that focuses on what is wrong rather than what is right. The news focuses on the negative rather than the positive because it is the negative that gets our attention; it is what sells. Our health care system focuses on illness instead of wellness and prevention. Many mental health care providers conduct sessions with their clients that involve focusing on their problems, and the self-help industry is a flourishing market for seminars, books, CDs and other programs that focus on improving or fixing that which we perceive to be wrong with us.

Having come this far in this book, it should be clear that what we focus on we attract into our lives. The challenge is that when we say we need to improve anything about our life, what we are really is saying is that we are not good enough. As long as we have the mindset that we are "not good enough," regardless of the area in our life, we cannot help but have resistance toward that area. If I want to improve my ability to be happy in life, then I am telling myself that there is something wrong with how I feel. Since I feel there is something wrong with how I feel, that is what I will be focusing on. It is for this reason that the Law of Attraction and self-help is incompatible.

The Law of Attraction offers insight to why it is difficult for most people to make a lasting change. Anytime we resist anything in life, we are engaged in a battle with that which we are trying to change. Change is difficult because we are battling ourselves all along the way. When we try to change who we are, we are fighting a battle against the universe. Our essential self is consciousness, and our manifested self is the physical form that we know ourselves by. As long as our focus is on what is wrong with us, that is what is being projected to the universe. The universe is vested in supporting us by manifesting in our lives that which we focus on. It is by manifesting what we focus on that the universe provides us with the opportunity for expansion, which directly benefits the universe. The only way to experience the life that we desire is to learn acceptance and self-love for who we are at this moment and focus on how we want our life to be.

The practice of mindfulness, or presence, is completely compatible with the Law of Attraction for that reason. Happiness can only be found in the present moment. As long as we believe that our happiness will come when we have achieved our goals, when our situation changes, or when life starts going our way, we will continue to fool ourselves. True happiness comes from discovering who we are at the essence of our being, which is changeless. Anything else that we are chasing is just an illusion. By learning to be mindful and loving ourselves, just as we are, all that we desire will manifest in our lives, though how it appears may differ from what we expect. Utilize the appreciation exercise from Chapter 2 to develop self-acceptance for your world and then focus on creating your masterpiece.

Chapter 10
When the Law of Attraction Pulls the Rug From Under You

Earlier in this book, an explanation was offered on how our subconscious thoughts can work against our conscious intentions when trying to manifest. However, there is another dynamic that can also lead to unexpected results. The dynamic that I am referring to is the conflict that we sometimes experience with our conscious mind and our desires. Sometimes we desire something for our lives, but we tell ourselves to ignore that desire. We rationalize why we should not pursue our desire, but our desire is stronger than our rationalization. The result is that the universe will comply with our desires in an unexpected way. When this happens, it is easy to confuse the universe's response as bad luck or misfortune. In truth, it is evidence of the universe supporting us. The following story offers an example of this.

Jon was a teacher, who had taught for seven years at the junior high level. Though he loved his job, his enthusiasm for the job began to wane as the years progressed. By the time he started his seventh year of service, he had started to entertain the idea of quitting teaching and going into a new career. He had grown tired of the discipline problems, the cutbacks in funding, and changes in administrative policy. Though we wanted to leave, he remained there as he felt it would be irresponsible for him to leave, given that he was the sole income earner for his family. Further, his wife would have gone crazy if he told her he wanted to leave; she was adverse to uncertainty.

While at work one day, Jon made a mistake that would cost him his job. A student acted out and was about to engage in a fight with another student. Jon lost his head and reacted by grabbing the student to prevent him from advancing toward the other student. Because of strict school policies regarding physical contact with students, Jon was fired on the spot. He was without a job, a seemingly major setback for him and his family.

By the following day, Jon was dedicating his time to looking for another job. He sent out resumes en masse, attended job fairs, and joined a networking group, but received no offers or interviews.

Jon was feeling stressed as his savings were rapidly dwindling. One day while meditating, Jon suddenly received a realization. When he was relaxed, and his mind was silent, he experienced a voice from within him telling him everything would be fine. When he woke-up from his meditation, he felt great, almost giddy. Nothing in his circumstances had changed; he was still without any job prospects, yet he felt great. This time, Jon approached his job search from a whole new state of mind. Rather than being worried, Jon had a knowing that he would find a job. The next day, he saw an ad in the paper for a position that he had never heard of before, a curriculum developer. As he knew nothing about what the job entailed, he looked it up on the internet and found the job description for the position. What he read excited him and he applied for the job. Jon got an interview and received an offer that very day. Jon loves his new job, and the pay and benefits for his family exceeded that of his old job.

Jon's story illustrates how the universe is always working to support us in achieving happiness if we are willing to listen. Your desires are messages from the universe or the larger consciousness. When we try to suppress our desires or rationalize why we should stay where we are, the universe will eventually step in if we are not willing to take action ourselves. Jon resisted following his desires. As a result, the universe pulled the rug out from under him. Jon's fears of being unemployed offered resistance to receiving his gift from the universe. It was only when he let go of his resistance, during his meditation, that he was able to attract into his life that fateful job posting. It was his continued sense of trust that allowed him to get hired.

We can think of our relationship with the universe, or the greater consciousness, as a circular feedback loop. Our desires are our connection with the universe, with our essential self. If we are not listening to our desires, the universe will make us listen. At that time, the universe will set into motion the people, circumstances, and events that will make us receptive to them.

The following is a meditation for when life throws you for a loop:

1. Sit down in a comfortable position, close your eyes, and breathe normally.
2. Place your attention on your breath by focusing on the sensations of it traveling in and out of your body.
3. As your focus on your breath, you will experience the appearance of thoughts. When they appear, simply ignore them and return your attention back to your breath.
4. If you keep your focus on your breath, there will come the point when you can maintain your awareness of it without any effort. When you reach this stage, think about how you would feel emotionally if you had the outcome that you desired? Experience these emotions as fully as possible.
5. Imagine what you would see if you had the outcome that you desired.
6. Imagine what you would touch if you had the outcome that you desired.

7. Imagine what you would hear if you had the outcome that you desired.
8. Make these experiences as real as possible, making them more intense whenever possible and then let them go.
9. When you are ready, awake from your meditation.

Chapter 11
Putting It All Together

We have covered a lot of information in this book, so in this chapter, we will discuss how to put all this information together so that you can develop a plan for creating the life that you desire. At the most basic level, there are two components that you need to practice to make effective use of the Law of Attraction. These components are intentions and resistance.

1. Intention: Your intentions are your projections to the universe of what you want to experience. Your projections should take the form of how you want your future to be like, not how things are in the present moment. If you focus on what you have now, you will just get more of it. If you focus on how you want it to be, that will be your experience.
    The following exercise will help clarify what to focus on: Write down the various categories of your life. Common life categories include the following:
    - Emotional
    - Relationships
    - Financial
    - Health

- Professional
- Spiritual

2. When you have your categories, rate each category according to your level of fulfillment with it, with zero being totally unfulfilled and five being totally fulfilled. The categories that have the lowest scores are where you may want to focus on first.
3. When creating a vision for a category, you want to see it the way you want it. These visions are your intentions.
4. When you have identified your intentions, the next thing is to discover why you are not living your vision today. To answer that question, ask yourself what has prevented you from living your vision today. The underlying answer to that question is resistance. Review Chapter 2 and choose the exercises for releasing resistance that you feel most comfortable with. I highly recommend that you learn meditation and the self-love techniques described in the chapter.
5. Regardless of which exercises you choose, practice them. Make them a daily practice until you can manifest them.
6. Remember that the essence of manifesting is developing love and appreciation by cultivating the feelings that are associated with these emotions. As you cultivate these emotions, express your intentions. When

you have done this, remain open to the manifestations that enter your life.
7. If you have more than one intention, you can focus on one intention at a time, or you can do several at a time, depending on how comfortable you are with the process.

Exercise for Changing a Belief

Changing beliefs that create resistance in our lives to beliefs that empower us is central to becoming a conscious manifester. Fortunately, there is a simple process for this.

Do the following:

1. Get two large pieces of writing paper (8" x 11" or larger).
2. Take the first paper and fold the paper in half-lengthwise so as to make two columns.
3. On the top of the paper, write down a belief that you want to change.
4. In the left column, list all the consequences you have experienced for having this belief. Examples could be how this belief has affected your relationships, your sense of self-worth, your emotional well-being, your health, or your finances, etc.
5. When you write your list, do not think about what to write; rather, write whatever comes to mind. Also, write as fast you can. The idea is to write from the heart.

6. When you have completed the list, assign a number to each item on the list. The number that you are assigning is a measure of how heavily this item has impacted you. The assigning of numbers is done purely arbitrarily, go by your feelings or the first number that comes to your mind.
7. When you have completed assigning a value to each item, total the numbers and record it at the bottom of the list.
8. In the right column, repeat this exercise, the only difference is that you are going to make a list of all the benefits you have gained from having this belief. As in the first column, assign a number to each item and record the total at the bottom of the right column.

For the second paper, you will repeat the exercise, except it is going to focus on the new belief that will replace the old one. Do the following:

1. Get two large pieces of writing paper (8" x 11" or larger).
2. For the first paper, fold the paper in half- lengthwise so as to make two columns.
3. On the top of the paper, write down a new belief that will replace the old belief. Example: If the old belief was "I never do anything right," your new belief may be "Every time I try something new I learn something."

4. In the left column, list all the benefits that you feel that you would experience if you lived by this belief. When you write your list, do not think about what to write; rather, write whatever comes to mind. Also, write as fast you can. The idea is to write from the heart.
5. When you have completed the list, assign a number, from zero to five, to each item on the list. The number that you are assigning is a measure of the amount of difference in your life that you believe that this item would make. The assigning of numbers is done purely arbitrarily, so go by your feelings or the first number that comes to your mind.
6. When you have completed assigning a value to each item, total the numbers and record it at the bottom of the list.
7. In the right column, you will repeat what you did in the left column, with one difference. You are going to make a list of consequences that you believe that your new belief may create. As in the first column, assign a number to each item and record the total at the bottom of the right column.
8. When you have completed the two lists, read each item from the lists, making sure that you allow yourself to experience the feelings that arise when reading it. When you finish reading the lists, compare the number totals from the two papers. By comparing the number totals,

you will be reminded of the weight that each of these lists has on your life.
9. Repeat step 8 each day until you feel that the emotional intensity for adopting the new belief has taken place.

Create a Planner

To help you organize all your information, create a Law of Attraction planner for yourself. There are Law of Attraction Planners on the market, or you can create your own. Your planner should include the following sections:

- A place to record your short-term goals

- A place to record your long –term goals

- The areas of your life that you want to improve in (see earlier part of this chapter).

- Your daily planner: For daily scheduling exercises from this book, action items, and other pertinent information.

- Your new beliefs (see exercise from this chapter).

- A note section where you can jot down ideas and insights.

Chapter 12

Sustaining the Effort

Learning to manifest takes time and patience. Because of this, it is easy to start doubting yourself or get off track and not practice the exercises. In this section, we will discuss ways to sustain your efforts, including trusting yourself, decision making, and support groups.

One of the major challenges in learning how to manifest is learning to trust your abilities, which can be a challenge if you are not experiencing evidence of your manifestation. For this reason, it is easy to doubt yourself. For this reason, it is helpful to start off by manifesting things that are not important to you. I will share a personal experience to illustrate this point. When I first started learning how to manifest, my intention was to increase my income. My reason for wanting to increase my income was in alignment with love, as I want to provide more for my family. After a week of meditating and expressing my intentions, I still did not see any change in my income, even though I did my part by taking all needed action. I found myself continuously looking for the slightest piece of evidence to confirm that the Law of Attraction was working. I started to doubt the Law of Attraction; my continuous looking for results was an expression of my lack of trust in my abilities to manifest.

When I realized what I was doing to myself, I changed my intention from attracting something that was emotionally charged, which was money, to making an intention to attract something that I was not emotionally attached to, which was a magazine. I thought of a magazine cover that I would see when I went to the library later that day. Sure enough, I saw the magazine cover that I visualized in my mediation. Because the magazine cover was not important to me, I did not spend time thinking about it. By continuing to practice in this manner, I developed the trust in myself to manifest those things that were emotionally significant to me.

Decision Making

Throughout our life, we need to make decisions about how we are going to move forward in our lives. How do we know that our decisions are aligned with the intentions that we are working to manifest? The following are guidelines for making decisions:

1. Ask yourself whether the decision that you make will bring you closer to your intentions or will it move you further away.

2. Rather than restricting yourself to making a certain decision, are there other choices that you could make? Rarely in life are we restricted to one choice.

3. Once you have made your decision, stick with it until a better choice presents itself. Until then, cultivate as many positive emotions as you can for your decision.

4. Show appreciation to yourself for making a conscious decision and investing yourself in it.

Support Group

As with any human endeavor, it is always helpful to be around people of like-mindedness who can support you, encourage you, and provide you feedback. There are many groups, both online and in-person, for those who share an interest in the Law of Attraction. Find a group where you can share experiences and information.

Words of Encouragement

As mentioned earlier, the Law of Attraction is not an end unto itself. The Law of Attraction is just a normal function of the universe that we are learning to use consciously. We want to learn to manifest because we believe we will be happier if he can attract our desires into our life. By attracting into our life that which we desire, we believe that we will feel whole, that we will no longer feel that we are missing something from our life.

Upon achieving higher levels of awareness, it will become evident to you that who we are is beyond your thoughts, beyond your concepts, and beyond your desires. As consciousness, you are the one that is aware of all these things. Who we are at our most essential level does not know the meaning of need, desire, effort, or manifesting, for we are the witness of it all. As pure consciousness, we can manifest anything we want spontaneously without effort. To reach your essential nature does not require you to learning anything new or to practice any skill. Rather, it involves letting go of your need to be anything other than who you are with full acceptance.

Don't forget to get your free eBook and join our newsletter to be notified about Maya's new releases at a discounted price + receive more bonuses and resources related to LOA and similar topics...

Sign up for free at:

www.YourWellnessBooks.com/affirmations

problems with your sign up?

Email: info@yourwellnessbooks.com

www.ingramcontent.com/pod-product-compliance
Lightning Source LLC
Chambersburg PA
CBHW071009080526
44587CB00015B/2404